1996 Examination Questions
Suggested Solutions

Law of Tort

LLB

University of London
External Examinations

Solutions by David Holloway
BA (Cantab), Barrister

HLT Publications

HLT PUBLICATIONS
200 Greyhound Road, London W14 9RY

ISBN 0 7510 0753 6

British Library Cataloguing-in-Publication.

A CIP Catalogue record for this book is available from the British Library.

Printed and bound in Great Britain.

CONTENTS

ACKNOWLEDGEMENT

The questions used are taken from the University of London LLB (External) Degree examination paper and our thanks are extended to the University of London for the kind permission which has been given to us to use and publish the questions.

Caveat

The answers given are not approved or sanctioned by the University of London and are entirely our responsibility.

They are not intended as 'Model Answers', but rather as Suggested Solutions.

The answers have two fundamental purposes, namely:

a) To provide a detailed example of a suggested solution to examination questions, and

b) To assist students with their research into the subject and to further their understanding and appreciation of the subject.

Note

Please note that the solutions in this book were written in the year of the examination. They were appropriate solutions at the time of preparation, but students must note that certain caselaw and statutes may subsequently have changed.

INTRODUCTION

Why choose HLT publications?

Holborn College has earned an international reputation for the outstanding quality of its teaching, Textbooks, Casebooks and Suggested Solutions to past examination papers.

Our expertise is reflected in the outstanding results achieved by our students in the examinations conducted by the University of London LLB Honours Degree Programme for External Students, the Council of Legal Education, and by students in over 70 universities who use our publications.

Suggested Solutions

The Suggested Solutions series provides examples of full answers to the problems posed by examiners. The solutions are much more than answers achievable by a candidate under examination conditions. The opportunity has been taken, where appropriate, to develop themes, suggest alternatives and set out additional material providing further comprehensive topical coverage.

To aid comprehension and revision, the solutions are fuller than would be possible under examination conditions. It is important to keep in mind that at this level there almost certainly is more than just one approach in answering any given question.

We feel that in writing full opinion answers we can assist you with your research and further your understanding and appreciation of the law.

Notes on examination technique

Although the SUBSTANCE and SLANT of the answer changes according to the subject-matter of the question, the examining body and syllabus concerned, the TECHNIQUE of answering examination questions does not change.

You will not pass an examination if you do not know the substance of a course. You may pass if you do not know how to go about answering a question although this is doubtful. To do well and to guarantee success, however, it is necessary to learn the technique of answering problems properly. The following is a guide to acquiring that technique.

Time

All examinations permit only a limited time for papers to be completed. All papers require you to answer a certain number of questions in that time, and the questions, with some exceptions carry equal marks.

It follows from this that you should never spend a disproportionate amount of time on any question. When you have used up the amount of time allowed for any one question STOP and go on to the next question after an abrupt conclusion, if necessary. If you feel that you are running out of time, then complete your answer in note form. A useful way of ensuring that you do not over-run is to write down on a piece of scrap paper the time at which you should be starting each part of the paper. This can be done in the few minutes before the examination begins and it will help you to calm any nerves you may have.

Reading the question

It will not be often that you will be able to answer every question on an examination paper. Inevitably, there will be some areas in which you feel better prepared than others. You will prefer to answer the questions which deal with those areas, but you will never know how good the questions are unless you read the whole examination paper.

You should spend at least 10 MINUTES at the beginning of the examination reading the questions. Preferably, you should read them more than once. As you go through each question, make a brief note on the examination paper of any relevant cases and/or statutes that occur to you even if you think you may not answer that question: you may well be grateful for this note towards the end of the examination when you are tired and your memory begins to fail.

Re-reading the answers

Ideally, you should allow time to re-read your answers. This is rarely a pleasant process, but will ensure that you do not make any silly mistakes such as leaving out a 'not' when the negative is vital.

The structure of the answer

Almost all examination problems raise more than one legal issue that you are required to deal with. Your answer should:

Identify the issues raised by the question
This is of crucial importance and gives shape to the whole answer. It indicates to the examiner that you appreciate what he is asking you about.

This is at least as important as actually answering the questions of law raised by that issue.

The issues should be identified in the first paragraph of the answer.

Deal with those issues one by one as they arise in the course of the problem
This, of course, is the substance of the answer and where study and revision pays off.

If the answer to an issue turns on a provision of a statute, CITE that provision briefly, but do not quote it from any statute you may be permitted to bring into the examination hall
Having cited the provision, show how it is relevant to the question.

If there is no statute, or the meaning of the statute has been interpreted by the courts, CITE the relevant cases
'Citing cases' does not mean writing down the name of every case that happens to deal with the general topic with which you are concerned and then detailing all the facts you can think of.

You should cite only the most relevant cases – there may perhaps only be one. No more facts should be stated than are absolutely essential to establish the relevance of the case. If there is a relevant case, but you cannot remember its name, it is sufficient to refer to it as 'one decided case'.

Whenever a statute or case is cited, the title of statute or the name of the case should be underlined
This makes the examiner's job much easier because he can see at a glance whether the relevant material has been dealt with, and it will make him more disposed in your favour.

Having dealt with the relevant issues, summarise your conclusions in such a way that you answer the question
A question will often say at the end simply 'Advise A', or B, or C, etc. The advice will usually turn on the individual answers to a number of issues. The point made here is that the final paragraph should pull those individual answers together and actually give the advice required. For example, it may begin something like: 'The effect of the answer to the issues raised by this question is that one's advice to A is that ...'

Related to the previous paragraph, make sure at the end that you have answered the question
For example, if the question says 'Advise A', make sure that is what your answer does. If you are required to advise more than one party, make sure that you have dealt with all the parties that you are required to and no more.

Some general points

You should always try to get the examiner on your side. One method has already been mentioned – the underlining of case names, etc. There are also other ways as well.

Always write as neatly as you can. This is more easily done with ink than with a ball-point.

Avoid the use of violently coloured ink eg turquoise; this makes a paper difficult to read.

Space out your answers sensibly: leave a line between paragraphs. You can always get more paper. At the same time, try not to use so much paper that your answer book looks too formidable to mark. This is a question of personal judgment.

NEVER put in irrelevant material simply to show that you are clever. Irrelevance is not a virtue and time spent on it is time lost for other, relevant, answers.

EXAMINATION PAPER

UNIVERSITY OF LONDON
LLB EXAMINATIONS 1996
for External Students
PART I EXAMINATION (Scheme A)
SECOND AND THIRD YEAR EXAMINATIONS (Scheme B)
GRADUATE ENTRY LEVEL II (Route A)
GRADUATE ENTRY SECOND AND THIRD YEAR (Route B)

LAW OF TORT

Wednesday, 12 June: 10.00 am to 1.00 pm

Answer *FOUR* of the following EIGHT questions

1 Maisie and Nigel live next door to each other in a row of terraced houses. Nigel works on night shifts and is studying for an Open University degree. He spends most days sleeping, studying or watching Open University programmes on television. Maisie has been licensed by the local council under statutory powers as a child minder and is permitted to look after up to ten children under five during the daytime from Monday to Friday. Nigel finds the noise of the children in Maisie's house and garden very distracting; it keeps him awake and makes it difficult to concentrate on the television programmes. He has taken to singing obscene songs in a loud voice. Some of the young children have picked up the words and the parents are threatening to remove them from Maisie's care.

Advise Maisie and Nigel.

2 'The law of England does not impose any general duty of care to avoid negligent misstatements or to avoid causing purely economic loss even if economic damage to the plaintiff was foreseeable. However, such a duty of care will arise if there is a special relationship between the parties.' (*White* v *Jones*, per Lord Browne-Wilkinson).

Discuss.

3 Tina and Una were sisters, aged 82 and 76. They had lived together in a ground floor council flat since Una returned from working abroad eleven years ago. Una began to suffer from Alzheimer's disease and Tina found it difficult to cope. She sought assistance from the council's social services department, who agreed in October to have special locks fitted to all the doors and windows so that Una would not be able to wander out of the house. Tina telephoned twice about it, but nothing was done. In February Una managed to open a window during the night and climbed out in her nightdress. Tina awoke to find Una missing and wakened a neighbour, who telephoned the police. The police telephoned the neighbour later in the day to tell them that Una had been found sitting in a bus shelter suffering from hypothermia and taken to hospital. She died before Tina was able to reach the hospital. Tina has suffered a complete mental breakdown.

Advise as to any possible tortious liability on the part of the council.

4 Geoffrey, a student, took a holiday job last summer as a gardener at Barsetshire Hall, a stately home owned by Lord Trollope. He was working one day using a rake which had been manufactured by Dudtools plc and recently purchased by Lord Trollope from a reputable supplier. When he had finished work, he discovered that the door of the toolshed had stuck. As he was in a hurry, he tried to pull it open using the prongs of the rake. After a few moments the shaft of the rake split and a large splinter pierced the palm of his hand. Because of a rare blood condition (of which he had until then been unaware), he suffered very severe poisoning and lost a year before he could return to his university studies.

Advise Geoffrey as to any causes of action in tort (a) against Dudtools plc and (b) against Lord Trollope.

How (if at all) would it affect your answer if Geoffrey had known of the blood condition and had told Lord Trollope at the time he took the job?

5 'Causation should be a matter of common sense and not of legal rules.'

Discuss with reference to the law of tort.

6 Discuss the issues of tortious liability which arise in the following situations:

i) Ben and Clive were members of staff of the Downland University and are both keen researchers and have published many books and articles. The Higher Education Funding Council is conducting a research assessment exercise evaluating the research output over the past four years of members of staff in post in universities on 31 March 1996. In November 1995 Upmarket University offered Ben and Clive appointments with substantial financial inducements if they took up appointment there on 1 March. Unusually for a university contract (where the normal period of notice is three months) Ben and Clive had to give six months' notice, but they resigned from Downland and accepted appointments at Upmarket on 1 March. Their research output since 1992 is therefore attributed to Upmarket University, and Downland University has received a low research rating and its funding has been severely reduced.

ii) Daphne owns several florists' shops. She obtains many of her supplies from a market garden owned by Edgar. She telephones Edgar each Friday to place her order for the coming week. Freda tells Daphne (correctly) that Edgar has a financial stake in a farm run by his brother, which exports live animals to the European continent. Daphne is very active on behalf of 'animal rights' and immediately notifies Edgar that she will take no more supplies from him.

7 During March and April 1996 the Daily Scum ran a series of articles each week in its children's section giving a profile of leading popular singers and groups.

One article featured a group called The BCDs, whose members are Bill, Con and Dan. The article included the statement: 'The BCDs are a group of amiable lads, but a bit wild. One of them was deported from Germany a while back because of some trouble at a concert.' Another article was about a vocalist, Evangeline. It included the statement: 'Evangeline has had an unusually long career. The photo shows her singing at a concert in Nirvana seven years ago.'

In 1994 German promoters had oversold tickets for a concert where the group to which Bill then belonged was to perform. The concert was cancelled and the group was asked to leave Germany but not formally deported.

Because of the imprisonment of a pop singer in Nirvana in 1988 other performers (including Evangeline) refused to go there until 1991 when the singer was released. The picture was taken in 1987.

Advise the Daily Scum as to any possible liability in defamation.

8 Gorgon Enterprises were building a new factory. For two weeks they hired a huge crane from Crane Co, together with its driver, Max. One day Max saw a group of boys spraying lorries on the site with paint from aerosol cans. He caught one of the ringleaders, Neil, aged 12, and pulled him down from the lorry. Neil fell heavily and banged his head. A blood clot developed and he suffered severe brain damage. He has still an expectation of life of 30 years but is unlikely ever to find employment.

Advise Neil's parents (i) whether there is a cause of action in tort and, if so, against whom, and (ii) how financial compensation should be assessed.

SUGGESTED SOLUTIONS

QUESTION 1

Maisie and Nigel live next door to each other in a row of terraced houses. Nigel works on night shifts and is studying for an Open University degree. He spends most days sleeping, studying or watching Open University programmes on television. Maisie has been licensed by the local council under statutory powers as a child minder and is permitted to look after up to ten children under five during the daytime from Monday to Friday. Nigel finds the noise of the children in Maisie's house and garden very distracting; it keeps him awake and makes it difficult to concentrate on the television programmes. He has taken to singing obscene songs in a loud voice. Some of the young children have picked up the words and the parents are threatening to remove them from Maisie's care.

Advise Maisie and Nigel.

SUGGESTED SOLUTION TO QUESTION 1

General Comment

This is a classic private nuisance problem involving two neighbours whose uses of their property are mutually incompatible. The question involves analysing the strengths of each side's potential claim in nuisance and the remedies available to each.

Skeleton Solution

Nigels's claim in nuisance:

- reasonableness, statutory authority, social utility;
- remedies.

Maisie's claim in nuisance:

- reasonableness, malice;
- remedies.

Suggested Solution

Assuming Nigel has the necessary proprietary interest there is a prima facie argument against Maisie. Noise is a type of disruption which is capable of amounting to nuisance: *Halsey* v *Esso Petroleum Co Ltd* (1). Nigel will need to establish that Maisie's conduct is unreasonable; however arguments that Maisie's conduct is socially useful, and that it has been authorised or licensed by statute will mitigate against this.

Considering the social utility of Maisie's conduct first, although this does not strictly speaking amount to a defence to a nuisance action (*Bellew* v *Cement Ltd* (2) and *Adams* v *Ursell* (3)) it will be taken into account when assessing whether or not Maisie's conduct has been unreasonable, and so a nuisance. Certainly the balance of utility here would seem to be against Nigel, as his study habits and requirements are a purely personal preference, whereas Maisie's conduct is of use to the community at large. Further, Nigel's wish to sleep during the day is idiosyncratic, and the law of nuisance will not protect an abnormally sensitive plaintiff: *Robinson* v *Kilvert* (4). On balance I would advise that on the face of it Nigel cannot complain that Maisie's conduct is unreasonable. This is of course subject to evidence about the noise levels, which may in fact be abnormally loud.

In addition to this, Masie may be able to rely on the fact that she has statutory licence to carry on her activities. The House of Lords case of *Allen* v *Gulf Oil Refining Co Ltd* (5) is the leading authority on this defence. In the *Allen* case villagers sued in nuisance for disruption caused by the construction of an oil refinery near their village. The construction had been authorised by statute. Although the statute contained no direct authorisation for the noise levels etc involved, the House of Lords held that this disruption was a natural consequence of the authorised act and held against the villagers. According to this authority, were Nigel to win on the reasonableness point Maisie would have to show that the noise levels were a natural consequence of the authorised act, ie childminding for up to ten children up to five years old. I would submit that Maisie would have no difficulty establishing this (subject again to the levels not being abnormally high for this size of a group of children) and for these reasons Nigel's claim would be unlikely to succeed.

Turning to Maisie's case, again noise is the problem and this is capable of being a nuisance (*Halsey*), and again Maisie will have to show that Nigel has been unreasonable in his conduct: *Miller* v *Jackson* (6).

In *Christie* v *Davie* (7) the defendant was so annoyed by the plaintiff's singing lessons next door that he was provoked into disrupting these by making noise. The deliberate nature of the defendant's conduct made it actionable in nuisance. Similarly in *Hollywood Silver Fox Farm Ltd* v *Emmett* (8) the defendant's malicious conduct in firing his gun to interfere with the breeding of his neighbour's foxes was held to be a nuisance. The contrasting case of *Bradford Corporation* v *Pickles* (9) has been distinguished, and it is submitted that the fact that Nigel is aware of the presence of small children and the fact that his language is obscene point to the conclusion that his conduct is both deliberate and malicious. I would advise Maisie that she has a strong claim against Nigel in nuisance.

There is no direct authority as to whether Maisie can recover damages for loss of business in nuisance, although there are dicta to suggest that loss flowing as a natural consequence of a nuisance may be recoverable: *Ryeford Homes* v *Sevenoaks District Council* (10). Since no business has yet been lost I would advise that Maisie seek an injunction against Nigel.

References

(1) [1961] 1 WLR 683
(2) [1948] IR 61
(3) [1913] 1 Ch 269
(4) (1889) 41 Ch 88
(5) [1981] AC 1001
(6) [1977] QB 966
(7) [1893] 1 Ch 316
(8) [1936] 2 KB 468
(9) [1895] AC 587
(10) (1989) 16 Con LR 75

QUESTION 2

'The law of England does not impose any general duty of care to avoid negligent misstatements or to avoid causing purely economic loss even if economic damage to the plaintiff was foreseeable. However, such a duty of care will arise if there is a special relationship between the parties.' (*White* v *Jones*, per Lord Browne-Wilkinson).

Discuss.

SUGGESTED SOLUTION TO QUESTION 2

General Comment

The quotation comes from a case involving so-called *Hedley Byrne* liability. The question involves analysing and discussing this type of liability, the main mechanism by which a plaintiff can recover for 'pure' economic loss. This is a discussion question – there is no 'right' answer – however it is suggested that time would be better spent discussing trends in the development of *Hedley Byrne*-type liability than on lengthy discussion of, for example, classification of damages, or the facts of complicated cases.

Skeleton Solution

Hedley Byrne liability.

Caparo, Smith v *Bush,* special relationships.

Negligent statements and beyond.

Recent cases, conclusions.

Suggested Solution

Traditionally a plaintiff could only recover for pure economic loss where he was owed a contractual or fiduciary duty by the defendant. Material damage, such as personal injury, which results from the defendant's tortious conduct will be recoverable, but damage which is purely financial cannot. The House of Lords decision of *Murphy* v *Brentwood District Council* (1), which overruled the earlier authority of *Anns* v *Merton London Borough Council* (2), has eliminated many of the grey areas as to what can be classified as economic loss as opposed to the financial implications of material damage, and the trend since *Murphy* has been restrictive, ie the courts have been more ready to classify a defendant's loss as purely economic, and thus to deny recovery in tort.

The main remaining situation in which a plaintiff can recover in tort for pure economic loss will be where he can bring himself within the scope of the House of Lords decision of *Hedley Byrne & Co Ltd* v *Heller & Partners Ltd* (3). The facts of this case related to liability for negligent statements, but in subsequent cases the ambit of the decision seems to have widened to allow recovery for pure economic loss as a result of a defendant's acts or omissions in certain circumstances. The development of this new area of liability may be at odds with the restrictive trend mentioned earlier.

The facts of the *Hedley Byrne* case were that the plaintiffs asked their bank to advise as to the creditworthiness of their client, as the plaintiffs were liable under contracts negotiated on behalf of their clients. The bank obtained a positive reference for the defendant company, and the plaintiffs relied on this. The reference had been carried out negligently and on the liquidation of the client company, the plaintiffs were liable for losses sustained under a contracts negotiated for the client company. The loss was purely economic in nature, and the plaintiffs sued on the basis that the defendants owed a duty of care to the plaintiffs in carrying out the reference. The House of Lords held that such a duty could exist. The decision establishes an exception to the rule that pure economic loss is not recoverable in tort. The hallmarks of a situation in which this type of duty will arise involve an undertaking by the defendant to the plaintiff, reasonable reliance on this by the plaintiff and a special relationship between the parties.

The reason behind attaching greater liability for statements in general than acts or omissions is that these can be potentially more far-reaching, ie because statements can reach the public domain with relative ease, and can be relied on by many people, the consequences therefore may be more far-reaching. Such liability has been criticised by inter alia Weir (4) who argues that the effect of imposing such a duty may be to give the plaintiff the benefit of a guarantee or insurance policy by the defendant against any loss the plaintiff may incur in dealing with third parties. This may be potentially unfair, as the defendant can be liable for losses sustained by a plaintiff acting on the advice of his statement, but cannot seek to recover any of the profits from a successful use of his advice. In other words, the relationship is not contractual and the defendant receives no consideration, but incurs potential liabilities.

It is important to remember that liability will only be incurred where there is a special relationship between the parties, and the nature of this relationship has been examined in more recent case law. In *Smith* v *Eric S Bush (A Firm)* (5) a surveyor who negligently carried out a survey on a house was held liable to the eventual purchaser of the house for damage to the property, despite the fact that the surveyor's contract was with the estate agents who were selling the house, not with the purchaser. The House of Lords held that a duty was owed by the surveyor to the purchaser because the relationship between the parties was 'akin to contract'. The reality of this commercial situation was that the purchaser had paid the price of the survey to the agents and that the surveyor was aware that the purpose of the survey was to enable the purchaser to decide whether to buy the house. Hence the parties had the necessary proximity to give rise to the special relationship mentioned. The purpose for which the statement was made was also held to be a relevant factor in the case of *Mariola Marine Corporation* v *Lloyd's Register of Shipping* (6). Here: a Lloyd's ship surveyor was held not liable to an eventual purchaser of a ship on the grounds that the purpose of the survey was to assess safety and seaworthiness of the ship, not to protect the economic interests of ship purchasers.

Similarly in the case of *Caparo Industries Ltd* v *Dickman* (7) accountants who had prepared accounts for the audit of a company were not liable to another company which mounted a takeover bid for the first company on the basis of the information contained in the negligent audit. The House of Lords held that the audits were in general circulation and were not prepared for the purpose of influencing third party decisions as to the sale or purchase of shares. So it would seem that the test requires a certain degree of proximity between the parties, and the court again will look at the purpose for which the statement is made. This is not the same as the foreseeability test as in both *Caparo* and *Mariola* it could be said that it was reasonably foreseeable that a third party *might* act on the information as the plaintiffs did in these cases. The test is a stricter one involving a special and deliberate relationship between the parties, such as employer and employee: *Spring* v *Guardian Insurance* (8); or Lloyd's name and agent: *Henderson* v *Merrett Syndicates* (9).

So far the cases discussed have involved negligent statements or advice, but the *Hedley Byrne* principle may extend beyond this sphere to impose liability for economic loss caused by negligent acts and omissions as well. In *White* v *Jones* (10) the House of Lords applied the *Hedley Byrne* principle and held that a solicitor was liable to the intended beneficiaries of his client's will. The testator had fallen out with his daughters and instructed his solicitor to cut them out of his will. After a subsequent reconciliation he instructed his solicitor to amend the will again in order that his daughters be given a legacy. The testator died before the will was amended but the House of Lords held that the necessary proximity and knowledge had been established and the defendant solicitor was therefore liable to the intended beneficiaries on *Hedley Byrne* grounds.

It is still unclear how far the *Hedley Byrne* principle will develop to cover loss caused by acts and omissions as opposed to negligent statements, but inconsistencies within the case law are emerging. The case of *White* v *Jones*, above, affirmed the earlier House of Lords decision in the case of *Ross* v *Caunters* (11) but *Ross* was decided on grounds of foreseeability. Thus the decision of an earlier case has been affirmed but using different reasoning. Similarly the case of *Pirelli General Cable Works Ltd* v *Oscar Faber & Partners* (12), which seems to have been decided along the lines of *Anns* v *Merton*, was referred to by Lord Keith in *Murphy* as a *Hedley Byrne* case. It is clear that the exact scope of this type of liability should be more clearly defined as it still cannot be stated with clarity whether the case of *Hedley Byrne* establishes liability for economic loss caused by negligent statements, or howsoever caused. There is also some tension between the recent expansive trend in this area of liability and the restrictive cases regarding classification of loss.

References

(1) [1990] 3 WLR 414 = Sparton Steel v Martin T.272
(2) [1978] AC 728
(3) [1964] AC 465
(4) [1963] CLJ 216
(5) [1990] 1 AC 831
(6) [1990] 1 Lloyd's Rep 547
(7) [1990] 2 AC 605
(8) [1995] 2 AC 296 T. 224
(9) [1994] 3 WLR 761
(10) [1995] 2 AC 207 T. 290
(11) [1980] Ch 297
(12) [1983] 2 AC 1

QUESTION 3

Tina and Una were sisters, aged 82 and 76. They had lived together in a ground floor council flat since Una returned from working abroad eleven years ago. Una began to suffer from Alzheimer's disease and Tina found it difficult to cope. She sought assistance from the council's social services department, who agreed in October to have special locks fitted to all the doors and windows so that Una would not be able to wander out of the house. Tina telephoned twice about it, but nothing was done. In February Una managed to open a window during the night and climbed out in her nightdress. Tina awoke to find Una missing and wakened a neighbour, who telephoned the police. The police telephoned the neighbour later in the day to tell them that Una had been found sitting in a bus shelter suffering from hypothermia and taken to hospital. She died before Tina was able to reach the hospital. Tina has suffered a complete mental breakdown.

Advise as to any possible tortious liability on the part of the council.

SUGGESTED SOLUTION TO QUESTION 3

General Comment

The facts of the question do not disclose any particular statutory obligation on the council's social services department to deal with elderly residents of council property who suffer from some form of mental disability. Thus, the most likely liability exposure for the council is in the tort of negligence, and for the purposes of this question, the tort of breach of statutory duty will not need to be addressed. At issue is whether the council is liable in negligence for the death of Una and for Tina's nervous breakdown.

Skeleton Solution

Introduction.

Duty of care.

Breach of duty.

Causation.

Foreseeability of damage.

Damages.

Nervous shock.

Suggested Solution

For the council to be liable in negligence for the death of Una, it must first be established that it owed her a duty of care to install window and door locks. While Lord Atkin in *Donoghue* v *Stevenson* (1) acknowledged that a duty of care encompassed the avoidance of omissions likely to cause harm, English law has traditionally been reluctant to enforce a duty of positive action (see the comments of Lord Goff in *Smith* v *Littlewoods Organisation Ltd* (2) and those of Lord Diplock in *Home Office* v *Dorset Yacht Co Ltd* (3)) in the absence of a 'special protective relationship', such as parent to child. The latter are very limited, but have included situations of 'custodial authority' – in other words, warders over prisoners, as in *Ellis* v *Home Office* (4); in *Kirkham* v *Chief Constable of Greater Manchester Police* (5), it was held that there was a duty of care to monitor suicidal prisoners – and in one case, that a school has a duty to ensure that a child does not leave the school grounds without a responsible adult: *Barnes (An Infant)* v *Hampshire County Council* (6). However, the courts have, on the grounds of public policy, been consistently reluctant to impose a duty of care of action upon government authorities in relation to their operational decisions. For example, in *Alexandrou* v *Oxford* (7) it was held that the police did not owe a duty to respond to 999 calls made by alarm systems. See also *Hill* v *Chief Constable of West Yorkshire* (8) and *Knight* v *Home Office* (9) for similar cases of immunity of public authorities from a duty of care.

Notwithstanding the above, it is argued that the council, by its promise in October, *assumed* a duty of care to Una, and should have installed the locks on the doors and windows. In *Bromley London Borough Council* v *Ellis* (10) a gratuitous insurance agent (ie, one acting voluntarily and not under contract) was held liable when he failed to inform a car owner that his auto insurance policy had failed: the agent had promised to act for the car owner. Similarly, in *T* v *Surrey County Council* (11), a child was injured by a council-approved child minder, against whom allegations of abuse had been made – the mother of the child had expressly relied upon the assurance of the defendant council that the minder was safe, and the council was held to be liable.

It is submitted that the council in this case, on the basis of these authorities, assumed a duty of care to Una to install locks on the doors and windows. Clearly they did not, and are in breach of this duty. However, it is also necessary, for there to be negligence on behalf of the council, for this breach to have caused the circumstances leading up to Una's death (*Barnett* v *Chelsea and Kensington Hospital Management Committee* (12)), and that her death by hypothermia was a reasonably foreseeable type of damage flowing from the breach: *Hughes* v *Lord Advocate* (13); *Overseas Tankship (UK)* v *Morts Dock & Engineering Co (The Wagon Mound No 1)* (14).

It is likely on the balance of probabilities that the failure to install locks caused Una's death – with them, she would not have been able to leave the flat and freeze to death in her disoriented condition. Similarly, there is no question that death by hypothermia was damage of a type reasonably foreseeable from the breach of duty owed to an elderly woman suffering from Alzheimer's disease in February in England.

Una's estate would be able to recover damages for pain and suffering which she experienced before her death, as well as funeral expenses under s1(1) Law Reform (Miscellaneous Provisions) Act 1934. Given Una's age and her Alzheimer's condition, it is unlikely that Tina is a dependent of Una – as such she would be unable to claim damages for loss of pecuniary benefit under s1 Fatal Accidents Act 1976, and as Una is neither a spouse nor a child, Tina would be unable to claim bereavement damages under s1A of the 1976 Act.

The next issue regarding the council's liability relates to Tina's nervous breakdown. Recovery for nervous shock (or psychiatric injury) by non-primary victims is very limited in its scope. There must be a recognised form of psychiatric illness due to the apprehension of a horrific event, or its immediate aftermath, caused by the negligence of the defendant, in which a suitably close loved one of the plaintiff is involved: *McLoughlin* v *O'Brian* (15); *Alcock* v *Chief Constable for South Yorkshire* (16). It is submitted that on the facts, Tina was not come within the scope of those requirements and that she is unable to claim damages for nervous shock.

In conclusion, the council is likely to be liable in negligence for the death of Una, but not for Tina's nervous breakdown.

References

(1) [1932] AC 562
(2) [1987] 1 All ER 710 at 729
(3) [1970] AC 1004 at 1060
(4) [1953] 2 QB 135
(5) [1990] 2 QB 283
(6) [1969] 1 WLR 1563
(7) [1993] 4 All ER 328
(8) [1989] AC 53
(9) [1990] 3 All ER 237
(10) [1971] 1 Lloyd's Rep 97
(11) [1994] 4 All ER 577
(12) [1968] 2 WLR 422
(13) [1963] AC 837
(14) [1961] AC 388
(15) [1983] 1 AC 410
(16) [1992] 1 AC 310

QUESTION 4

Geoffrey, a student, took a holiday job last summer as a gardener at Barsetshire Hall, a stately home owned by Lord Trollope. He was working one day using a rake which had been manufactured by Dudtools plc and recently purchased by Lord Trollope from a reputable supplier. When he had finished work, he discovered that the door of the toolshed had stuck. As he was in a hurry, he tried to pull it open using the prongs of the rake. After a few moments the shaft of the rake split and a large splinter pierced the palm of his hand. Because of a rare blood condition (of which he had until then been unaware), he suffered very severe poisoning and lost a year before he could return to his university studies.

Advise Geoffrey as to any causes of action in tort (a) against Dudtools plc and (b) against Lord Trollope.

How (if at all) would it affect your answer if Geoffrey had known of the blood condition and had told Lord Trollope at the time he took the job?

SUGGESTED SOLUTION TO QUESTION 4

General Comment

The question raises issues of Lord Trollope's liability as an employer and also issues of manufacturer's liability for defective products. The final part of the question requires consideration on issues of contributory negligence and volenti.

Skeleton Solution

Dudtools' liability.

– under the Consumer Protection Act 1987 and at common law;

– defences.

Lord Trollope's liability:

– safe plant and equipment;

– volenti and contributory negligence.

Suggested Solution

Geoffrey will wish to show that Dudtools plc are liable for the defective rake. One should first look to the Consumer Protection Act (CPA) 1987 to see if Geoffrey is afforded any statutory protection by it. The rake is clearly a product or 'goods' for the purposes of s1(2) of the Act, and the loss suffered, personal injury, is also covered under s5(1) of the Act. Geoffrey will then have to establish that the damage was caused wholly or partly by a defect in the rake. The standard laid down in s3 of the Act is that the safety of the product must be such as 'persons generally are entitled to expect'. One of the relevant factors in assessing whether the product has achieved this standard is 'what might reasonably be expected to be done with ... the product'. It is here that Geoffrey may experience some difficulties, for it would seem that the rake was not manufactured for the purpose of opening jammed doors. It is arguable, however, that the rake might be expected to be robust enough to cope with general wear and tear of work in the garden. A lot would depend here on the individual facts of the case, eg whether the rake was a plastic garden rake or a heavier hay rake. In any case Geoffrey will have to establish that his injuries are a result of a particular defect in the rake, and not his application of too much force on the rake.

Assuming Geoffrey would be able to establish this, we will consider the defences available to Dudtools. Section 4 of the Act lays down a number of statutory defences to an action for defective products. None of these defences seems to be applicable here. The development risks defence laid down in s4(1) has regard to the state of scientific knowledge at the time of manufacture, but this relates to the defect in the rake, not to Geoffrey's condition, and would be irrelevant unless the defect was caused by something very obscure and untraceable. The defence of volenti would also be inapplicable – as Geoffrey was not aware of the extent of the risk of poisoning, he could not have consented to it. The key issue here is what caused the injury: was it Geoffrey's carelessness, or a defect in the rake? Were it to be the former, Geoffrey would not recover, and were it to be the latter Dudtools would have no defence. The evidence points to a conclusion half way between these positions, ie that the injuries were caused by some defect in the rake, coupled with some fault or carelessness on Geoffrey's part. I would advise, then, that Geoffrey would recover a reduced amount of damages in an action against Dudtools, by virtue of the Law Reform (Contributory Negligence) Act 1945. There is also a possibility of a common law action against Dudtools on *Donoghue* v *Stevenson* (1) principles. However, if anything the standard of care required at common law from a manufacturer is lower than that required under the CPA 1987 (hence the raison d'etre of the Act itself) and so Geoffrey's case would be no stronger. Had Geoffrey known of his condition I would submit that this would have the effect of weakening his claim against Dudtools, as he should have taken more care in the circumstances.

Geoffrey's claim against Lord Trollope will be governed by the duty of care owed by an employer to his employee. The extent of this duty was defined most notably in *Wilsons & Clyde Coal* v *English* (2). One aspect of this is the duty to provide adequate plant and equipment. Geoffrey will argue that there has been a breach here in that both the shed door and the rake constitute defective plant and equipment. The standard of care required of an employer is the same as that in negligence, ie he is required to take reasonable care, effectively therefore Lord Trollope is obliged to inspect and check the equipment thoroughly enough to spot a defect: *Murphy* v *Philips* (3). It may be the case that the defects would not have been discoverable even on a thorough investigation, in which case Lord Trollope would not be liable – this argument would seem stronger in relation to the rake than to the door. Again much will depend on the circumstances surrounding the injury, but there is an arguable case that the equipment is defective.

Assuming Lord Trollope has been in breach of the duty outlined above, the question arises as to whether the loss sustained is too remote a consequence of the breach, as the blood condition is unknown to Lord Trollope. Although Lord Trollope could not have predicted the extent of the injuries caused, due to his ignorance of Geoffrey's condition, the so-called 'eggshell skull rule' will apply here. The rule dictates that as long as some damage to the person is a foreseeable consequence of negligence it generally does not matter that the precise nature and extent of the damage were unforeseeable: *Dulieu* v *White & Sons* (4). A narrower approach was taken in *Tremain* v *Pike* (5) where the plaintiff contracted Weil's disease while employed by the defendants. The disease is very rare and caused when human beings come into contact with rats' urine. There was no evidence that the defendants were aware of the possibility of the disease being contracted and it was held that the defendants were not liable as the damage suffered was 'entirely different in kind' from that which could have been foreseen by the defendants. The Court of Appeal has more recently disapproved this decision in the similar (contract) case of *H Parsons Ltd* v *Uttley Ingham & Co* (6). Lord Denning stated in *Parsons* that the issue of foreseeability applied equally in contract and tort, so this case would imply that the damage suffered by Geoffrey would not be considered too remote in that some injury would be a foreseeable consequence of the provision of a defective door or rake, if it can be established that Lord Trollope failed to inspect the equipment adequately.

As with Geoffrey's potential claim against Dudtools, the court may choose to reduce damages because of Geoffrey's partial fault under the Law Reform (Contributory Negligence) Act 1956, and will reduce the amount according to the relative fault of Geoffrey, although the courts apply this provision reluctantly in employment cases: *Caswell* v *Powell Duffryn Associated Collieries* (7), which indicates that Geoffrey may fare better in his action against Lord Trollope than against Dudtools in this respect. Finally, had Geoffrey known about his condition this would work against him only as regards the defence of volenti. Had he not known of the disease the defence cannot be established, as he could not consent to a risk he knew nothing about. Where he knew about the condition it is arguable that he knew of the risk and therefore assumed it. This presumes, however, that Geoffrey's knowledge of his blood condition extends to the knowledge that a splinter would cause him such severe poisoning, which would seem unlikely.

Furthermore the courts are reluctant to allow the defence of volenti in employment cases (*Smith* v *Baker & Sons* (8)) as employees may be under understandable pressures to accept risks at work which they would not normally accept in other situations. This would make it less likely that Lord Trollope could establish a defence of volenti, although Geoffrey's knowledge could increase the court's assessment of fault on his part, and thereby reduce the damages.

References

(1) [1932] AC 562
(2) [1938] AC 57
(3) (1876) 35 LT 477
(4) [1901] 2 KB 679
(5) [1969] 1 WLR 1556
(6) [1978] QB 791
(7) [1940] AC 152
(8) [1891] AC 325

Cook v *Lewis* leads into one of the thorniest problems in the law of causation, that of the standard of proof. In *McGhee* v *National Coal Board* (8) an employer was held liable in negligence for an employee's contraction of dermatitis. The House of Lords held that the employer's failure to provide washing facilities had *increased the risk* of the employee contracting the disease. It was never established that the lack of facilities had actually caused the disease. This case was subsequently applied by the Court of Appeal both in *Wilsher* v *Essex Area Health Authority* (9) and in *Fitzgerald* v *Lane* (10). In both cases the defendants were held to be liable in negligence, and in both the plaintiff established only that the defendant's conduct had *increased the risk* of damage occurring (not that the conduct had actually caused the damage). Slade LJ referred in *Fitzgerald* to the fact that it would have been impossible in that case for the plaintiff to prove that the defendant actually caused the loss. The Court of Appeal seemed to be mitigating the harshness of the rules of causation, particularly in medical cases where it is often impossible to pinpoint the precise cause of a disease, the justification for this being 'broad justice'.

The tensions between the certainty of legal rules and the application of notions of fairness and justice in hard cases, or judicial discretion, is apparent in these decisions. The House of Lords has subsequently retreated from a liberal interpretation of *McGhee* in a line of cases including *Kay* v *Ayrshire and Arran Health Board* (11) and *Hotson* v *East Berkshire Area Health Authority* (12). The culmination of this process was the House of Lords decision in the *Wilsher* appeal (13). This reversed the Court of Appeal decision and established firmly that in all cases the plaintiff bears the burden of proving on the balance of probabilities that his loss was caused by the defendant. Lord Bridge added that any attempt to use the decision in *McGhee* to modify this principle was 'fruitless'.

It would seem then that English law has adopted a rule-based approach to the issue of causation rather than a common-sense approach. This certainly has the advantage of certainty, however as technology advances it may become more and more difficult to establish liability against doctors, employers etc because proof of causation will become too difficult to obtain, and this may be a recipe for results which offend against common sense. The courts seem to have opted out of the debate, wishing to avoid a haphazard uneven development of the principles of law in this area. Perhaps this is a question which the legislature should consider.

References

(1) [1952] 2 All ER 402
(2) [1969] 1 QB 428
(3) [1962] 1 QB 33
(4) [1962] 1 WLR 295
(5) [1988] AC 175
(6) [1970] AC 1004
(7) [1952] 1 DLR 1
(8) [1973] 1 WLR 1
(9) [1987] 2 WLR 425
(10) [1987] QB 781
(11) [1987] 2 All ER 417
(12) [1987] AC 750
(13) [1988] AC 1074

QUESTION 6

Discuss the issues of tortious liability which arise in the following situations:

i) Ben and Clive were members of staff of the Downland University and are both keen researchers and have published many books and articles. The Higher Education Funding Council is conducting a research assessment exercise evaluating the research output over the past four years of members of staff in post in universities on 31 March 1996. In November 1995 Upmarket University offered Ben and Clive appointments with substantial financial inducements if they took up appointment there on 1 March. Unusually for a university contract (where the normal period of notice is three months) Ben and Clive had to give six months' notice, but they resigned from Downland and accepted appointments at Upmarket on 1 March. Their research output since 1992 is therefore attributed to Upmarket University, and Downland University has received a low research rating and its funding has been severely reduced.

ii) Daphne owns several florists' shops. She obtains many of her supplies from a market garden owned by Edgar. She telephones Edgar each Friday to place her order for the coming week. Freda tells Daphne (correctly) that Edgar has a financial stake in a farm run by his brother, which exports live animals to the European continent. Daphne is very active on behalf of 'animal rights' and immediately notifies Edgar that she will take no more supplies from him.

SUGGESTED SOLUTION TO QUESTION 6

General Comment

Both of these questions ask the candidate to address torts within the sphere of unlawful interference with trade, in the context of specific situations. The first one calls for a discussion of the tort of inducing breach of contract, and the second one asks for a more thorough examination of the various component torts in this area.

Skeleton Solution

i) Inducing breach of contract.

Knowledge of existence of contract and intention to breach.

Inducement.

Breach caused loss.

Damage.

Justification.

ii) Unlawful interference with trade.

Conspiracy.

Inducing breach of contract.

Intimidation.

Suggested Solution

i) At issue is whether Upmarket University, in luring Ben and Clive, has committed the tort of inducing breach of contract, and if so, what remedies are available to Downland University.

The tort of inducing or procuring breach of contract has its origins in the case of *Lumley* v *Gye* (1). It encompasses situations where the defendant – lacking any justification – persuades or offers inducement to a third party to breach their contract with the plaintiff, causing damage to the plaintiff; the defendant must have knowledge of the existence of the contract and intend for the breach to take place: *Merkur Island Shipping Corp* v *Laughton* (2). For Upmarket to have committed the tort, each of these ingredients must be present.

Thus, Upmarket must have known of the existence of Ben

and Clive's contracts of employment, and have intended that they be breached: *Merkur Island*. The fact that a contract of employment exists between these two and Downland is obvious; for Upmarket to have intended Ben and Clive to breach the agreement, it is necessary for Upmarket to know of its terms. In businesses where the standard terms of the contract are well known, constructive knowledge of the terms will be imputed to the defendant: per Neill LJ in *Middlebrook Mushrooms Ltd* v *Transport and General Workers Union* (3).

We are told here that the customary notice period for an academic is three months, and that Ben and Clive's period of six months is exceptional. It is thus arguable that the only term of which Upmarket will have constructive knowledge is the usual three-month notice period; if Upmarket does not have actual knowledge of Ben and Clive's six-month period, then it will not have committed the tort, as it will not have intended them to breach their contracts.

Clearly, Ben and Clive have breached their contracts with Downland.

If Upmarket did have knowledge of the six-month period, it must next be proven that they used some degree of direct persuasion to convince Ben and Clive to breach their contracts with Downland: *Thomson* v *Deakin* (4). This component has been manifestly established, given that we are told the two received substantial financial inducements.

Finally, Downland must have suffered damage as a result of the breach of contract for the tort to be made out: *Exchange Telegraph Co* v *Gregory & Co* (5). The loss of funding due to Downland's poor rating, due to Ben and Clive's breach, would be sufficient for this purpose.

If Upmarket has committed the tort of inducing breach of contract, any attempt to raise justification – ie that it has some moral or legal right to procure the breach – as a defence would likely fail. Among the things which the court will assess when considering the applicability of this defence are the relative status of the defendant and plaintiff, and also the object of inducing the breach: *Glamorgan Coal Co* v *South Wales Miners 'Federation* (6). It is most doubtful that the wealth of Upmarket, combined with its motives in these circumstances would afford them the defence of justification. Downland could thus claim from Upmarket all damages which flow from the breach, which may be higher than those for a simple breach of contract: *Lumley* v *Gye*. In this case, Downland would be able to recover the funding lost as a result of its poor research rating.

ii) At question here is whether Daphne or Freda could be liable for the torts relating to unlawful interference with trade, which is to say the unlawful interference with the economic interests of another, other than by false representation: *Allen* v *Flood* (7). (We are told that Freda's comment is true, so there can be no grounds for any action based upon the tort of deceit, which deals with misrepresentations.) These include the torts of conspiracy, inducing breach of contract, and intimidation.

The tort of conspiracy involves either an agreement between two or more people to do an unlawful act, or to do a lawful act by unlawful means: *Mulcahy* v *R* (8). The purpose behind such a conspiracy must be to damage the plaintiff's business: *Crofter Hand Woven Harris Tweed Co* v *Veitch* (9). In this case, there is no agreement between Daphne and Freda to do anything unlawful, so the tort of conspiracy has not been committed.

The fact that the relationship between Daphne and Edgar is not a contractual one, and that there is no evidence to suggest that Freda intended Daphne to discontinue this relationship, would imply that the tort of inducing breach of contract cannot be established on these facts.

The tort of intimidation involves the existence of an intention to injure the business of the plaintiff, combined with the existence of an unlawful threat, which could include a crime, tort or breach of contract: *Rookes* v *Barnard* (10). While Daphne may have intended to injure Edgar's business by taking her business elsewhere, in the absence of a contract to the contrary this is not unlawful. Thus, she has not committed the tort of intimidation, as she is merely doing what in law she is entitled to do: *Ware and De Freville* v *Motor Trade Association* (11).

It is therefore submitted that Edgar has no cause of action in tort against either Daphne or Freda.

References

(1) (1853) 2 E & B 216
(2) [1983] 2 AC 570
(3) [1993] ICR 612 at 612
(4) [1952] Ch 646
(5) [1896] 1 QB 147
(6) [1903] 2 KB 545
(7) [1898] AC 1
(8) (1868) LR 3 HL 306
(9) [1942] AC 435
(10) [1964] AC 1129
(11) [1921] 3 KB 40

QUESTION 7

During March and April 1996 the Daily Scum ran a series of articles each week in its children's section giving a profile of leading popular singers and groups.

One article featured a group called The BCDs, whose members are Bill, Con and Dan. The article included the statement: 'The BCDs are a group of amiable lads, but a bit wild. One of them was deported from Germany a while back because of some trouble at a concert.' Another article was about a vocalist, Evangeline. It included the statement: 'Evangeline has had an unusually long career. The photo shows her singing at a concert in Nirvana seven years ago.'

In 1994 German promoters had oversold tickets for a concert where the group to which Bill then belonged was to perform. The concert was cancelled and the group was asked to leave Germany but not formally deported.

Because of the imprisonment of a pop singer in Nirvana in 1988 other performers (including Evangeline) refused to go there until 1991 when the singer was released. The picture was taken in 1987.

Advise the Daily Scum as to any possible liability in defamation.

SUGGESTED SOLUTION TO QUESTION 7

General Comment

The problem requires an application of the relevant aspects of defamation. The law should be applied to the relevant facts and the paper's potential liability to Bill, Con, Dan and Evangeline considered.

Skeleton Solution

Libel – slander – publication.

Liability to B, C and D – defences.

Liability to E – defences.

Suggested Solution

The classic definition of defamation was made in the case of *Youssoupoff* v *Metro-Goldwyn-Mayer* (1). It is the publication of a statement which tends to lower a person in the estimation of right-thinking people generally or makes them shun or avoid him. Any defamatory statement in a permanent form is a libel, whereas a defamatory statement in a non-permanent form is a slander. Thus as both articles in the Daily Scum are in writing, if defamatory they will constitute a libel rather than a slander. This will mean that if Bill, Con, Dan or Evangeline can establish that the statements are defamatory, they need not show special damage, as libel is actionable per se.

In order to establish the tort of defamation according to *Youssoupoff*, the plaintiff must show that:

a) the statements were published;

b) the statements referred to the plaintiff;

c) the statements were defamatory in the sense outlined above.

It would seem evident that requirement (a) is satisfied in both instances as publication means simply communication to a third party: *Bata* v *Bata* (2).

Considering first the story about The BCDs, can the band members establish requirements (b) and (c) above? There are two parts to the story, first that the group are a bit wild, and second that one of them had to be deported from Germany after some 'trouble'.

Regarding the first part it is questionable whether the label 'a bit wild' would tend to lower members of a pop band in the estimation of people generally, in fact it may be the case that the group's reputation may be enhanced by this sort of publicity, unless the group's image was particularly clean cut. On balance I would argue that this part of the story is not defamatory. The second part of the story is more problematic. In fact none of the members of the band was deported from Germany, and the incident behind this part of the story does not seem to have involved any fault on the part of Bill, whereas the story seems to suggest that something illegal had happened, and that one member of the band had been in trouble with the authorities in Germany. This is more likely to do some damage to the reputation of the band than general 'wildness', and I would submit it to be defamatory on balance. Another problem with this part of the story is establishing whom it refers to. Although Bill was the only member of the band who was involved at all in this incident, the other members will be justified in arguing that the article refers to them by implication. This has been held to be sufficient in the case of *Le Fanu* v *Malcolmson* (3).

Although *Knupffer* v *London Express Newspaper Ltd* (4) makes it difficult for a member of a group to sue in respect of a statement about the group itself, the House of Lords held that this would be possible if the statement was capable of referring to the plaintiff, and indeed was understood to refer to the plaintiff. Furthermore, where the group is limited in size, the statement will be more likely to be held to refer to one of its members in such a case: *Brown* v *D C Thomson & Co* (5). I would submit that all the members of the band would be able to argue that the Daily Scum's article was libellous.

Although Bill was not actually deported, s5 Defamation Act 1952 states that the truth of every single item of the statement need not be proved 'if the words not proved to be true do not materially injure the plaintiff's reputation'. However, I would submit that the article is not at all founded on truth and so the Daily Scum will not be able to use the defence of justification.

To establish the defence of fair comment, ie that the story was fair comment on a matter of public interest, the paper will have to establish that the article was both an expression of opinion and that this opinion was based on true facts. In *Dakhyl* v *Labouchère* (6) a doctor was branded a 'quack of the rankest species' which was held to be fair comment, but again although every fact need not be proved true (s6 Defamation Act 1952) I think that in this case the paper has commented on untrue facts, and the story is based on a falsehood. To sum up then, I would submit that there are no defences available to the paper and that each member of the band may sue in defamation for the second part of the story.

Regarding the potential claim of Evangeline, it is submitted here that there will be no difficulty establishing that the statement was published, and in this case refers to Evangeline, but was it defamatory? The words in the article relating to her career are inoffensive on the face of it. The problems lie with the juxtapositioning of her photograph alongside the text claiming that the picture was taken seven years ago in Nirvana. This statement about the photograph is false and may lead people to believe that Evangeline was not taking part in the boycott of Nirvana at the relevant time. Although the words in the piece are, on the face of it, inoffensive, to the reader who knows about music and the music business they could tend to damage Evangeline's reputation. Evangeline has to establish here what is known as 'true innuendo', ie that additional facts known to the reader give the piece an additional and defamatory meaning. According to *Hartt v Newspaper Publishing Ltd* (7) the court in these circumstances should have regard to the hypothetical ordinary reader who is neither 'naive nor unduly suspicious' and the test is whether the article would lower the plaintiff in the estimation of such a reader. There are two arguments here: firstly that the readership of a children's magazine is sensitive and aware of human rights issues such as these, on the other hand as the protest ended five years ago, many readers will be too young to remember these events; although secondly it must be added that it is not only children who may read the children's section – it is possible that many of the readers of the main newspaper may read the children's section and make the necessary connection. I would conclude that although this is an arguable issue, on balance it is likely that the article would have damaged Evangeline's reputation in the eyes of the readership of the children's section, and therefore true innuendo and defamation could be established by Evangeline.

Regarding defences, as in the first instance I would advise that the incorrect dating of the picture will rule out both the defences of justification and fair comment for the reasons given above, as this is not a trivial mistake of fact, but one which goes to the heart of the issue of defamation. There is no evidence, however, to suggest that the story was maliciously published or that it was activated by malice. The Daily Scum may therefore wish to argue that the story was innocently published under s4 Defamation Act 1952. To succeed with this statutory defence they will have to establish (s4(1)(b)) that:

a) the words were not defamatory on the face of them;

b) the Daily Scum was unaware of circumstances that would make them so; and

c) they had used all reasonable care.

It would seem possible that the dating of the picture was a simple unintentional error and I would advise, pending further evidence as to the procedures used by the paper in checking and researching these stories, that the defence may succeed. In which case my advice to the Daily Scum would be to publish a correction and apology to Evangeline under s4(3) Defamation Act 1952 as soon as practicably possible. If the paper could establish that it had taken reasonable care, then Evangeline's rejection of such an apology would amount to a defence to libel. Although the section would not apply to the story about The BCDs, as the statement in that case was defamatory on the face of it, I would advise the paper in that case to print an apology and correction as soon as possible and make an offer of amends under either RSC O.22 or s2 Defamation Act 1952: although this will not amount to a defence against an action by the group, it will have the effect of mitigating damages.

References

(1) (1934) 50 TLR 581
(2) [1948] WN 366
(3) (1848) 1 HL Cas 637
(4) [1944] AC 116
(5) 1912 SC 359
(6) [1908] 2 KB 325n
(7) (1989) The Times 9 November

QUESTION 8

Gorgon Enterprises were building a new factory. For two weeks they hired a huge crane from Crane Co, together with its driver, Max. One day Max saw a group of boys spraying lorries on the site with paint from aerosol cans. He caught one of the ringleaders, Neil, aged 12, and pulled him down from the lorry. Neil fell heavily and banged his head. A blood clot developed and he suffered severe brain damage. He has still an expectation of life of 30 years but is unlikely ever to find employment.

Advise Neil's parents (i) whether there is a cause of action in tort and, if so, against whom, and (ii) how financial compensation should be assessed.

SUGGESTED SOLUTION TO QUESTION 8

General Comment

The first question calls for discussion of the tort of battery, and its potential overlap with the tort of negligence, and any defences available. It also requires an examination of the principles of vicarious liability.

The second question asks for a general discussion of the remedy of damages and the various heads of damages available to Neil.

Skeleton Solution

i) Battery.

Negligence.

Ex turpi causa non oritur actio.

Vicarious liability.

ii) Damages:

- general;
- special.

Suggested Solution

i) At issue here is whether Neil will have a cause of action in battery or negligence against Max, and whether he would also have an action against Gorgon Enterprises and/or Crane Co.

Battery is the direct, intentional (or, possibly, reckless) infliction of unlawful physical force upon another person, who does not consent to such touching: *Letang* v *Cooper* (1); *Wilson* v *Pringle* (2). Where the force is inflicted unintentionally, or indirectly, then an action in negligence will lie: *Letang* v *Cooper; Fowler* v *Lanning* (3).

It is submitted that Max has committed the tort of battery, as the force which he inflicted upon Neil was direct and intentional. In *Poland* v *John Parr & Sons* (4), it was held that employees can use reasonable force in the protection of their employer's property – however, it is argued that the force used by Max in these circumstances was not reasonable, and there is an issue as to whether Max is an employee of Gorgon (see below).

Similarly, s3(1) Criminal Law Act 1967 allows anyone to use reasonable force to prevent the commission of a crime, such as criminal damage, in this case. Again, it is contended that Max has used unreasonable force in these circumstances, and that this statutory defence is therefore not available to him.

Max could try to plead the defence of ex turpi causa non oritur actio, which means that the defendant should not benefit from his guilty act. Thus, in *Pitts* v *Hunt* (5), a drunken person riding on the handlebars of a motorcycle was held unable to recover in negligence from the driver – his criminal act was held to have caused his injury. In this case, it is submitted that ex turpi would not apply, as the injury was not caused by Neil's unlawful activity, but rather by Max's use of force.

Max will be liable for the full extent of Neil's injuries – it is immaterial that they are more severe than could reasonably have been foreseen.

As Max's financial resources may be limited, Neil's parents may wonder if Gorgon Enterprises or Crane Co could also be sued. The general rule in law is that an employer will be vicariously liable for the torts of his or her employees committed in the course of their duties. There is no question that Max is an employee of Crane Co, but it is not so clear whether he can be considered one of Gorgon. Generally speaking, employers will not be liable for torts of their independent contractors. In *Mersey Docks and Harbour Board* v *Coggins & Griffiths (Liverpool) Ltd* (6) a crane operator and his crane were 'lent' to a firm of stevedores. In the course of the operation, he negligently injured a third party. It was held that though the stevedores had the ability to direct what sort of work should be done, the stevedores did not have the ability to direct *how* the work would be done. As such, they were not in *control* of the crane operator and he was therefore not their employee. It is submitted that a similar situation exists here, and that Max is only an employee of Crane Co and not of Gorgon.

For Crane Co to be vicariously liable to Neil, however, it must also be established that Max was acting within the course of his employment. This will be a question of fact, but a good guideline was given by Salmond and Heuston (7) to the effect that a servant will be acting within the course of his employment when he performs a wrongful act authorised by the master, or the act is a wrongful and unauthorised *mode* of performing an act authorised by the master.

It has been held that an employee acting on his own initiative, as Max appears to have been doing in this case, *can* be acting within the course of his employment. In *Poland* v *Parr*, it was held that an employee could be acting within the scope of his employment where he genuinely believed that his employer's property was in danger, and used force to protect the property. However, in Max's case, the lorries were not his employer's property.

If Crane Co had expressly or impliedly given Max a discretion to act in this manner when the property of others was threatened, then he could be construed as acting within the scope of his employment: *Smith* v *North Metropolitan Tramways Co* (8). Whether or not this is the case is not clear from the facts of the question, and this is doubtful, given that his primary role was to operate the crane. In *Warren* v *Henlys Ltd* (9), the employer of a petrol station attendant was held not to be vicariously liable when he assaulted a customer in an act of personal vengeance – the garage has given no such discretion to the employee.

It is submitted that in pulling Neil off the lorry, Max acted out of the scope of his employment, and that Crane Co would not be vicariously liable.

Thus, Neil's parents should be advised that Neil would have an action in battery against Max, but not against Gorgon. They would also need to be informed that it is unlikely they would be able to sue Crane Co for Max's tort.

ii) Neil's parents should be advised that the function of damages in English law is to compensate the plaintiff for the pecuniary and non-pecuniary loss which flows from the tort. Neil will be entitled to general and special damages.

General damages are those which are said to flow directly from the tort itself, and which do not need to be specifically pleaded in a case. In general damages, Neil could claim for non-pecuniary loss, including pain and suffering and loss of amenity. Neil will be able to claim damages for any pain and suffering which he has experienced or will experience as a result of the accident, or necessary medical treatment: *Cutler* v *Vauxhall Motors Ltd* (10). He will also be able to claim damages for loss of amenity, which is to say enjoyment of life: *Lim Poh Choo* v *Camden and Islington Area Health Authority* (11).

Such damages will usually be awarded as a single lump sum – the quantum of these damages changes over time, and guides such as Kemp & Kemp's *Quantum of Damages* would need to be consulted for a guide to the general amount.

Special damages refer to the particular damage which results from the unique circumstances of the case, and need to be specifically pleaded. For example, Neil could claim financial losses between the date of the injury and trial, but would need to claim them as special damages (though he is unlikely to have lost any earnings, so the only damages of this kind are likely to be medical expenses).

Other special damages which Neil can claim from Max can be divided into two broad heads:

a) *Future losses resulting from the injury*
This means that Neil can be compensated for his loss of earning capacity in the future. This compensation will be assessed based upon a number of factors, including Neil's future employment prospects, his enduring incapacity for the future, and the number of working years which he has lost: *Taylor* v *O'Connor* (12).

To assess an amount for pecuniary damages, the court will derive a figure which is said to represent what Neil's annual earnings would have been in the future – the multiplicand – and will multiply it by the number of working years which he has lost – the multiplier. Deriving the multiplicand for a young boy of Neil's age may be difficult and arbitrary, but a court will still do so with children: *Housecroft* v *Burnett* (13) (though with older children, on the verge of a career, the multiplicand will be higher). With regard to the multiplier, we are told that Neil has an expectation of life of 30 years, but in reality a court will scale this figure down, to take into consideration such contingencies as unemployment and sickness. Once the figure is received, standard amounts will also be deducted for items such as income tax and other payments Neil would have made to the government such as national insurance contributions. Similarly, certain government payments, such as disability allowances, would need to be deducted (but not payments under private insurance policies). The aim will be to ensure that Neil is compensated, but that he is not overcompensated.

b) *Future medical expenses*
These will include payment of any kind of future medical expenses which Neil may have, such as medication, nursing care, etc. He could also claim compensation if members of his family had to give him care: *Croke* v *Wiseman* (14).

References

(1) [1965] 1 QB 232
(2) [1987] QB 237
(3) [1959] 1 QB 426
(4) [1927] 1 KB 236
(5) [1990] 3 WLR 542
(6) [1947] AC 1
(7) *Salmond and Heuston on the Law of Torts* (21st ed 1996), p443
(8) (1891) 55 JP 330
(9) [1948] 2 All ER 935
(10) [1971] 1 QB 418
(11) [1980] AC 174
(12) [1971] AC 115
(13) [1982] 1 WLR 71
(14) [1981] 3 All ER 852